Our Dark Academia

D1593098

RESCUE PRESS

CHICAGO | CLEVELAND | IOWA CITY

OUR DARK ACADEMIA
Copyright © 2022 Adrienne Raphel
All rights reserved
Printed in the United States of America
FIRST EDITION

ISBN 978-1-7348316-4-1

Design by Sevy Perez
Timberline & Adobe Caslon Pro
rescuepress.co

Our Dark Academia

Adrienne Raphel

TO MY COHORTS

1.

2.

3.

4.

*

1.

DAILY LIES

First, I wept.

I watered the ficus.

I cleaned the follicles.

First, I entered my name into the daily form and declared myself clean.

What does this mean?

Please do not ask, other people have grievous issues.

What is the highest good?

To sweat without procrastination.

How many things are necessary to know, to live and die happily?

Three, but which three will change.

I have graded everything. I am saving everything. I have started the day reading. I will end the day practicing. I will turn down the assignment because I do not need to add to whatever is hanging over my head.

Grant me the serenity to save everything except the things which I cannot. O I save everything I just cannot seem to save up.

First, I refused to see him.

The queen is in need of a husband. The crown is in need of a wife. The wonderful agents in Tom Ford masks will mail you branded wine. Books, but really old books they have to have vellum.

Lines 1–4:   Opening Lines

"Daily Lies," a play on "lines," and Our Daily Bread. If these are all
lies, the poem throws the relationship between speaker and reader
immediately into jeopardy. What the reader does in the poem might
directly contradict what she does in reality. Why would anyone lie about
these tasks? And yet, we know from the first that they are not true. What
are they masking?

Ficus to follicles to form, alphabetical progress. "The daily form,"
indicating the repetition. The plant, indicating growth. The hair, hair.

Lines 5–10:   The Catechism

Like a child asking why this night is different than all other nights, the
poem escalate the solitary splendor into a question-and-answer patter. The
questions lift their religiosity from the internet.

Lines 6–12:   What We Do to Self-Soothe

"Three, but which three will change" suggests: 1) That there are three
things rotating, one at a time, and which three will change is outside the
speaker's control; 2) That the rotation comes in groups of three;
3) Remember this poem has lies, and is this one of them?; 4) Three "firsts"
here, the poem lives the fiction of starting anew.

Lines 13–14:   And Then There Were None

Divided in fourteen segments roughly the length of lines, the poem drips sonnet. "First, I refused to see him" introduces a relationship between the speaker and the "him," someone exported from outside the poem's bubble. A dangerous relationship—is this the lie that tells the truth, or is this the lie that tells the truth?

DOMESDAY BOOK

Make a list of all the things you don't intend to do
My anxieties are gathering in my groin
Is it a muscle strain or a pull or a tear
Is it a hernia or a hysterectomy
Or astronomy or a wandering womb
My landlady thinks I'm hysterical, which, well

This fibroid is growing, the thyroid enlarging
They will not be able to operate it here
They will have to birth Prince Caspian elsewhere
Since they will have to cut me open vertically
It's true, he will ride out, fully formed, armor-clad
In stainless steel and cashmere cap, what a lad

I arranged this whole movement and now I don't want it
The student-led calvary thousands on thousands
A phalanx of youth skintight shining armor
But all of them dead, with the silence of hoofbeats
Of thronging ghost horses filling the courtyards
That they land (when they land) nowhere at all

The baby is stillborn the mother is laughing
It's now I'll admit he was never my child
I'll never be married, I thrust in anxiety
My legs wide on stirrups, the forceps prod in
To pull out the wire that makes me a woman
And pardon the muscle from sinew to smoke

OUR DARK ACADEMIA

In my ears the girls are just learning they are witches.
Blowing out candles with their minds, fluttering lights,
making cakey makeup melt off the jealous ones
to moonfed fleshy faces, pockmarked constellations;
our Quartet—Brooke, Vivian, Louise, Sylvia—
our Dark Academia, Artemis aesthetic, perfect skin.
They're getting bitchier, they lean into it,
burn the pillowcases with lacey cigarette butts,
and when the prefect (this is British boarding fantasy,
rotting vines, menstrual blood) challenges at lights-out
they point as one to a sneak smoke by the matron
doing laundry on a Sunday, which is the Lord's work.
They all of course share a secret which the rest of us
would die to know and so I sacrifice myself.
Today, waiting, hands chapped, stomped feet, at the reflecting pool,
me tiptoeing to stare at their eyes in the water,
I can hear them but they can't me, I'm not real
to them in the way that they're too real. In the way
they step back and it's not a reflecting pool but
a deer, round bloke eye rolling crazily out of its socket,
in the way of everything but don't touch it.
—All of them long dead in that first pandemic winter.
So I make them live it again, and again,
and I put on their blazers and smooth my face into theirs,
this past will overtake us because it already is.

STRESS SHOP

Spent half tonight on hands and knees
Searching for an earring, found the backing
Where I thought I might but it's still gone.
It was a cameo, old face, new to me
It cost something. I can feel it,
Phantom erring, where it should have been.
Could I *tell* you a more boring story?
I lost a ring months ago, in that old country,
And I ordered a replacement
Lo, but weeks later my mother dug it from the bag of carrots.
Back to the roots, my ring for a finger.

Everything here is an earring and a face,
Oat flake, dust mote, lint snarl, hard shell, flint bit, small rock,
Opaque pebble, convoluted plastic bits.
Whenever I lose jewelry it often comes back to me,
Not always, but I am good at finding coins.
Penny-wise, pound-foolish
I can go spinning to nowhere now. How many tabs
Can I keep open until the memory is too full
I just turn off the notifications.

Wrong number but I hope you lose
This is why I can't have nice things.
Though all my tabs are Things:
Amethyst heat blanket, heat blanket, therma jewel,
Helios the heated stone lounge
That molds to your glutes and thighs as you sit.
It remembers you, adjusts its heat to you.
You can have one thing in this life,
Working heat or working laundry.

Spent half tonight among the curlicue dust
Searching for an error, found the back.
Did I tell you my grandma tested positive
And out of nowhere I'd actually seen her
So I had to tell everyone I'd seen, all three of them,
Clean as chlamydia,
I drove up to this CVS and passed my swab through like a bank deposit
Except no one returned a lollipop

What else is new. Stress Shmoop. Dress shirt.
Boil stones in butter and you may sip the broth.
I buy vermillion, cotillion,
And I can sometimes get an orgasm all by myself,
Shut my eyes and it glows faster pastel,
Monet on the Tilt-a-Whirl,
Money I've just swirled away
If I don't find it and if I do.

MEMENTO MORI

Surely the only way to ensure immortality is through stuff.

Odette is stockpiling ten-year diaries. She has seven of them and she's thirty, so she'll live to a hundred.

Emily is buying memento mori rings, Georgian heirlooms from the Spanish Flu. Coral flowers and crystal skulls with diamond eyes, blue enamel on gorgeous gold bands. "Til death do us part, a romantic wedding or anniversary gift to remember the survivors of Covid in 2020, a reminder that if you can survive this, you can make it through anything together. A thoughtful gift to someone who has lost loved ones, for a funeral, especially to those who have lost parents in this pandemic."

Viv is buying futures, whatever that means, and bonsai from the internet, and lip balm in tiny neon plastic cheeseburgers, and she just set up a recurring donation to a marionette theater.

Mar is bookmarking pants in elaborate materials for if our lower halves ever materialize. I'm obsessed with this on the RealReal! Calen, 3.1 Philip, Chloe, and Olivia.

J. decks out her patio with a table that's exactly the size of the deck, a coffin. Two kinds of pie, pumpkin and ghost pumpkin, and ruff puff and mulled wine and crisp slaw and short rib and silver trays and white fur throws.

> *The girl stood on the driftwood deck*
> *Whence all but she had fled;*
> *The candles glowed in jars of Weck*
> *Where yeast-fed cultures bred.*

Grandma's selling the Nakashima, maybe it's time to die. The auctioneer laps it up. It's a hot market! He'll pay for the shipping, and the photographs, and any cleaning, and his commission is so low. The butterfly table, did you know what a rare specimen this is. We watched it sucked out through the screen, whoosh.

Me? I'm buying crystals. Aqua marina, brave heart it doesn't mean, but sailors swear to it as protection against stormy seas. Emerald, that's for universal and unconditional love, I wear it on my littlest finger. Citrine, stone of insight, joy to anyone starting a business. Sapphire, that's for wisdom. Black onyx is a weird energy, unbridled, princess of the night.

MIMI DU BIARRITZ ON HER BIRTHDAY

My name is Mimi du Biarritz and I make figurines
Here are my tweezers, I use the gold-plated Tweezerman needle-thin
Here are my safety pins for pricking

This one is Peggy Sue on a date with a zombie, it's like a regular person
But see here his torso is ravaged

Here is a bee storm engulfing this ballet dancer

Here is a cracker jack soldier living inside this mushroom

Oh and here is a little toy soldier in an actual mushroom cloud
See under the black tar the arm of a little child he is saving

Look here is a school under this glass specimen jar
I did the lawn in actual grass

I used astroturf for this school for the dead
Varsity letter sweater green felt

Here is a loofa criticizing the lettuce

Here is another inflatable palm tree because I stuck the first one by accident
With a bad safety pin

Here I did a mirror glacé for the South Pole
Arctic explorers and polar bear penguin parties
Which yes I'm mixing glaciers here
Antarctica is holographic sunglasses

And that's the tiniest reindeer fur in the world I stitched into their collars
Smuggled from the Nordic

Oh and this is a reef
It's the Great Barrier Reef, don't tell but it's
Out of actual reef I wasn't allowed to import

This crystal ball's from Rocky Mountain crystal
From above the tree line, do not touch, I got lost
For three days on the way down, the crystal
Re-magnetized everything, set the compass free

Oh this is a perfectly articulated St. Ann's Day feast

Here is a malachite succulent stretched into thin light
Reaching towards the idea of sun

It's a pearly gray day inside this snow globe
Which is a terrarium for a terrified dwarf tortoise
I keep little, call Ivan, he's sensibly scared

Here is a woman and her tiny fig tree
Tiny to the scale of the woman

Here is a figure skater mid-twirl
Gyroscope girl in the ice, a little shard of mirror
Today is her birthday, so every day is her birthday
So everything that she does, which is spin on one foot,
The other foot tucked figure-four into her knee,
Is always happening on her birthday

WHY ARE YOU SO NERVOUS

The baby's the size of a VHS tape
and the fibroid's the size of a grapefruit.
Quora already knows about the fibroid.
Oh, I've heard about your fibroid.

We've narrowed it down to the top three Lambs.
Just buy all three, says Quora, missing the point
entirely. It's not just any Lamb,
this will be Prince Caspian's Lamb!

What are you nervous about right now, says Quora.
Stop signs. Stairs. Ordering food.
Hair. Curling irons. My friend coming back.
Updated: multiple left turns.

Shading my hand from the sun I saw her from across the street
across the street. So glad of my glasses
darkening on their own, glad of the black mask.
When should I not be nervous about her.

Maybe it's when I'm having the baby,
not just pretending in the poem to have J.'s baby
and actually looking up iridescent egg dye
gold shimmer, those copper dippers.

NAMES 2.0

I was also going to be named after Arnold.
I hate the name Arnold thank god I wasn't a boy.
My brother was going to be called Hollis if girl.
Thank god, I hate the name Hollis.

Hollis is the name of the library system at Harvard,
Harvard All Souls Internal Revenues.
They have a free class on taxes but it's over before they tell you.
Trailing clouds of credit unions where'er I go.

Odette is the name of the librarian at Harvard.
She has a permanent position, envy and terror of us all.
I will not be an Odette. How do I get to be Odette.
Odi et amo. I don't know how to get out.

I found the timer function in this update.
Two more days before internal deadlines.
Two more days before the baby is a dude date.
Denali Moosetracks used to set up slacklines between two trees.

In the time when there were trees.
Ball pits. Odors. Chuck E. Cheese.

FELIX BY PROXY

We'd arranged to meet under the High Line,
Outside the Whitney; I was running down from
This photo shoot in Chelsea so I had
My clothes stuffed into a hiking backpack
And I was naked except for stilettos.
Felix was coming from choir practice.
He was tall, very thin, ginger-nut hair,
A two-vest situation, naked below the knees.
Hi, I said, glistening from the running;
You must be J.'s friend. Shall we fuck?
The ginger nut didn't say anything, eyes white.
I stuck out my hand. He looked at my updo. Hi,
He said. I'm in three choirs, did J.
Tell you? One's way in Harlem, that's the one —
I like best, the other two down here, one at this church
In Tribeca, the other one's sort of Midtown?
He had this soft, moony Irish brogue.
Two women in actual pillbox hats, tweed suits
Wheezed past me on their way into the museum.
A bus divulged tourists.
Another wave of day campers, Day-Glo T-shirts.
Wonderful, I said. Shall we fuck on the High Line?
He looked at the Hudson River. I'm—seventeen?
Fuck. I sighed. Okay. I shifted
My backpack, the straps were cutting into me.
I walked Felix to the 1 train. We parted,
He to Harlem for rehearsal, I to
My phone. At that point, Mar was just
Breaking up with Roman, the condom king,
Could I have him? What happened with J.'s guy,

Mar wrote back. Nope. I'm naked below
Eighteenth Street, I texted Roman,
But he must have been underground, it didn't send,
The line going from blue to green to red.

ON TATSE

The spine says The Physiology of Tatse and I have owned this mistake for a decade. Am I a non-taster?

I want a dog. I've never wanted a god before, I tell Emily.

To play handbells, every person gets one bell and you have to chime it in your specific time. So: Claire get G and Shannon gets G but an octave higher, and Greg gets E and Ross gets E flat and D because he can handle two of them and David who is the most advanced gets A and B flat and B. The way to play is by pointing to each letter and the person rings the bell, and a grueling melody comes out so sweetly, thick and treacly.

I play simultaneous chess with the grading, in the composition comments: HELEN As a reader I find your motive AYMAN your thesis relies on subjective opinion rather than objective HANNAH claim based on a scholarly argument As a reader RYAN I need more orienting avoid LEVI using the passive voice JONATHAN has been suspended.

At this stage I am very elaborate in my routine of things I need to do all day. I live to level up.

Dear AMY and RAPHAEL We would like to extend an invitation to join the symposium on the digital humanities. Please reply no later than.

The six senses: sight, hearing, smell, taste, touch, physical desire. The four humors: black bile, yellow bile, phlegm, blood. The four temperaments: melancholic, choleric, phlegmatic, sanguine. The five tastes: sweet, salty, sour, bitter, human. The ten plagues: sweat equity. If only there were only ten.

ALPHABET OF SPIES

A is for the elephant. B is for the
Blood. C I'm cold, put on a sweater,
D is never done. E is real elephant.
F it is for FUN. A is back and elegant
and G is here for gun. Hi I am for hire,
I for sure, apply. J for sure I am this job.
K and L I lied.
M it is Monopoly. O and then who died.
P and Q have spoiled you
R let's take a ride.
Simon Says the parents
These ones up for grabs
Understand what we have told you
Very very grand. Grandma's feeling
Excellent, don't tell her that she's done.
Anything you're raising to
The zeroth power's one.

EMILY EMPTY GIRL

It's a weird day astrologically, duh.
Friday the Thirteenth, don't bother.
This lifetime lifebulb, blown. A dead deer
Just out the peripheral. The deadest swallow
Falls out the leaf pile into the half-strewn street.
Empty Girl has rebranded as Emily.
She's got a sour stomach, thick sulfur,
Churning like a Martian lake
Tylenol versus aspirin. What Emily Girl
Does versus what she says she does. Nothing
Is wrong, the same temp but the light is insane.
Please be advised Emily Girl
No longer accepts tickets to her brain.
Happy birthday except it's tomorrow.

SINGAPORE MAGIC DREAM HOUSE

Mask up, underwear down. The gynecologist
doesn't get it but it's funny. The island's
100 km around, we bike it
in a day. Don't take that road today,
that's the tomorrow road, I'm saving it.
I had a little house, it was white as snow
But grunge-pink in the city, and it had to go.
We put an offer on the little house,
broke the no-carpet rule! but we are
the backup offer, for if the other's off.
Rihanna was supposed to come to campus
and instead she's got her backup dancers.
If you get lost in these woods
your fingerprint knows your concerns.

TYPHOID AUNT

Typhoid Aunt is hosting a party
An intimate lunch, just aunties and girl cousins
And Grandma and the other grandmother
They clean the Rose Room very beautifully
But look now they will let us have Rosalie Porch
Of course you'll come now it's outside

Typhoid Aunt is on a trip
She only goes to two places back and forth,
Just to her house in the south and her house in the north
Except to breakfast with Grandma
And to get brain-colored manicures

Oh Grandma wants a walk again
On the Boardwalk she never needed visit before
And now it's her only artery
Like a chute bombing candy to kids

Oh Nurse Donna caught it and stopped working
Days after she'd spread it to Grandma
The worst is not having what you don't know
Typhoid Aunt is having a nap
Now that I'm an influencer I have a vibe

Oh the plague is arranged inside any of us
Impersonal, like a baby
You have quite a collection of people you see
Unfair to live in the suburbs and don't want
To know I feel fine about anything
I worry a lot but at distance

THE RING

Be not afeard, he's very grounded, the apartment is full of tinctures and shit, but I was so old when I lost my virginity, I was losing my teeth. Losing a tooth during intercourse is a very powerful thing! What you do is plant it in the floorboard, and every night he dreams of teeth—teeth yellowing, teeth glowing white as milk, real fangs, plastic fangs, drugstore dentures, gumball teeth, tattoo teeth, invisible braces that aren't invisible—until you stop thinking about him, and then rootless he doesn't exist.

Monday's child is on time
Tuesday's child is a crime
Wednesday's child does what's ought
Thursday's child's on boycott
Friday's child up in flames
Saturday's child is to blame

I first lost the ring under his bed and he slithered more than half-naked to retrieve it. What if it took root: it would grow a ring tree, very fast over his bed, and as he sleeps the rings slither around him night after night, one by one, all ten toes, then knuckle by knuckle along his fingers, then the wrists, elbow, neck, knees, dick, dream of pharaoh—he'd never let the ring stay planted, he hasn't got a green thumb, he'd let the copper rot away and he'd left with the rust of it.

Knicker bocker, knuckle knocker
Run from your garden run
When you walk you walk on thorns
And erupt in corns and bunions

I soon lost it again, I didn't hear it fall, I traced the ground with my palms, dismantled my bag and my sweater and my body cavity but it wasn't anywhere, I gave it up for lost but years later I pulled it out from my hair.

King and Queen of the old boudoir
How many roads to Excalibur
One and one and one are three
When judgment comes where will you be

One time I was watching the cat of a woman who hated me and the cat bolted out the door, I ran out calling it by its name, I halted electrocuted just inside the door, the cat quivered, if I moved it would run away forever but if I stayed and let it make the first move it would still be both here and gone. I slipped but just a little but it was enough. The cat skittered, but only to under the house, and it glared at me. I put out my hand to make it stay there, to come to me. I got a bowl of milk, cats like milk?, and poured it thick so it glowed in the cat's eyes, the cat's whole back haunches tensed, but never moved. I tensed, but never moved. Years later the woman came back, too weary for this world, in one take swooped an arm under, scooped out the cat, swept off, the cat gloated.

Luminous cat, where are you at
The bell pull is frayed and broken
And the woman has fallen all broken
They all came tumbling after

Numinous cat, where did you go
Up top of the old church tower
But not the church where you last saw her
The bells, the bells are flying

Here is the ring your brother will use to propose to his wife! But the ring is too big for anyone's finger, and the ring has so many diamonds, she won't need all of them, they can use some of the diamonds to set into a new band, and you can use two of them to make into earrings! Maiden aunt, I cried, the better to hear you with.

Georgie down the wishing well
Wishing won't get Georgie well
Years, years later what a smell
Rhymes with playful not with hell

I'll marry myself!, a coppery ring around the pupils of my eyes, like someone with real liver failure, will I have me! I'll bear myself, and be born.

Better to fear you than lose you
Better to have than be choosey
Nothing to see here but surface
Blast it for diamonds and druse

RAINBOW RAINBOW RAINBOW

At the cemetery I did basic maths.
How much older was Mary than Douglas?
How much older was Stacey than I?
Robert, my father's birthday, but how many years.
Is there more traffic today than usual,
The one-eyed man croaks. I genuinely don't know.
The best tomb here is clearly RAINBOW.
Humor, Genius, Joy. Kids nowadays have names
Like pets. That feels wrong to say, but
I never had a babe. Would you be my
Faculty adviser? Are you my mother?
No one here will see me infect them
Which is the only reason I protect them.
How did I let the fish go? Only the dead know.

2.

FISH BOWL

All - just sent video of things Grandma does not want to take to her new apartment- she is def moving to Brightview in Devon early January. it's all very exciting and she's thrilled. If anyone wants any of these items please email or text me by Saturday. Otherwise going to goodwill. Will need you to pick them up at her apartment and we have couple months before the apartment sells.   Let me know and I'll put aside what you want as I'll be back down a couple times next week [heart heart]

A — grab all of Grandma's glass dishes, glass bowls, and the clear glass drinking glasses. Plus the glass xmas tree. I think a drive down there this weekend is in order to nab the stuff!

HEY

Some of it can be for you —I just want A to be our mule

Omg the video aunt P just sent
Grandma talking about how C likes to be in charge [tears of joy]

We will take two wine glasses and maybe a serving bowl

Be specific in your orders! grab those 4 gorgeous wine flutes, too!

A — you better jump on this — things are going fast!

Hi aunt P! Thanks for letting us know and giving us the opportunity to be able to keep some of these things [smile] i would love the flower dish at the very beginning of the video as well as those glasses with the little bubbles at the bottom, if no one else feels too strongly about them. I've been wanting to take a trip down soon anyway so I will be happy to do that [smile] [heart heart heart]

Ha - I'll let you and your sister split. You both wanted a couple same things. I'll put them aside and you guys can split up between you [heart-eyes]

Hi Aunt P! J and I are interested in those champagne flutes, along with one of the glass serving bowls. We'll get A to pick them up for us soon [smile]

Haha, sounds about right! Thank you! [smile]

Got off a conference call so just seeing this now. If they haven't already been claimed I'd like the oversized TV remote, any older issues of TV Guide and that scary ass red light in the guest bathroom

Hi aunt P! Thanks for texting us this! K and I would like the brown bowl towards the back and that starfish looking plate next to it. As well the clear cake plate towards the back as well

Whatever is left that's not trashy I'll take

Lol

This is the best comment [heart-eyes]

Love you all and I'll make piles for everyone when down there Tuesday!!!! Grand mom will be thrilled

You know what I like lol

Can I also claim the wooden bowl and dishes in that bowl in the second video? Thank you!

Yes!!! Have everyone's preferences and will pack up accordingly - except for the red light!

EXCUSES

I had to see the art across state lines
I had to eat the seaweed snax in gif
I had to run and do another exercise
I had to get a high from Snoop Dogg's spliff

The family's been cursed, in the old country
I protested, got arrested, just for being daughter
First mother, then my brother, now it's me
I tried to trick-or-treat, got sprayed with holy water

I have to order checks from the exchequer
I have to wash the dishes all by hand
I have to burn my eyeballs to my heckler
I need a better hobby, contraband

My output high but limited to zilch
The more I say I do the less I do
The more I worry the more I bitch
I sleep less and less but wake later too

THE STRAT

What color is persimmon?
What's up! I am Rebecca-Louise. I am your Executive
Obliques. Persimmon is a warm color.
You are Cool. Hi! Aquamarine-Lavender,
I am Bootcamp. Press Reboot.
What color is Rebecca-Louise?
Hi! I have been on hiatus but I am back.
This is your Rebecca-Louise Surprise.
This is a Cabernet-Sauvignon,
Now I go by Peloton.
Hi, what color is a pancreas?
What season is Purdue? Please?
Hi! Welcome to The Strat now.
Don't dillydally! Things you actually want are on sale.
Ten things The Strat can't live with or without:
The Strat recommends this squirrel-chipmunk ring.
Fifty-three teenagers vouch for hydration.
The Strat recommends that weighted blanket.
Do you bidet yet? Yay
Yes hi! Ten out of would recommend.
What we love about the holiday gift guide.
For the work wife. For the weighted thigh.
A dog crate from Fable a custom tiny house from
Modern Living and a globe is a very good deal.
What do we have? Desk, lamp,
Plants, stick-and-poke macramé,
Nothing is anywhere. Where do boxes go?

MIDNIGHT CALISTHENICS

Hi what's up it's Chrissie! I'm so glad you
Decided to spend this journey with me.
I will make this totally easy just listen to me.
Do everything I say to do and this will be totally easy!
I need you to feel supported. I need you to get enough grit
Underneath. I need it to get gritty. It's cold this morning
I put on this half-hoodie which if you know me
You know I don't usually! Have you ever tried
A bath bomb? It totally made my morning
I love it when you make time for yourself
Oh my god you have a dog too that is so sweet
Hold it hold it that's great! If you incorporate this
Into your routine that's great! Or if this your only workout of the day
Good for you for getting moving! Really good for you.
If you don't have a dog that's okay too!
You're doing this for you. If you like this check out more of me.
I have a whole series of these on demand. Also I have a book coming out
So great! I need you to hold on now. Hold it hold it
Come on, you're on my toes. Come on now. Three two one okay!
Towel off, hydration station. Love it. Do you.
That's a milestone! You know those things, pumice stones,
Oh my god, game changer! After this you have to do a dry rub.
You have to do a diffuser. You have to do oh we're back in the interval
Push it go! Hold it. Ok that's the way. Yes you! You're looking great just
Move up a little suck it in, yes it's going to get real results.
It's getting real! Yes you, you chose to carve out this moment for you.
No one else gets this time just for you. Hey I'm Chrissie thanks
For joining this journey with me. I'll see you all the time.

REAL ESTATE

It just got real real. Got royale.
It just got. I signed for it. What is a month?
An Essential Service. What is a vowel?
I owe you. What is a mouth but another part?
What's this state like? Just like any other
and a minibar. Half my life
has gone into this year! I'm angry
but my eyes are not very expressive.
—*My* eyes are *very* expressive. I went straight
for a two point five million bedroom,
a home theater, planetarium,
and an espresso machine. Damn.
And a chalet. Stop looking, stop it,
what am I going to do with my tabs.

STUDY
Hello, I'm everybody.
My name is the same as yours,
Backwards, with different letters.
You need to, I'll know yours.

HALL
I know you're going to stay.
You have nowhere else to go.
What, will you rent a revolver
With nobody anyone knows?

LOUNGE
—How grand! I've got that mint suit,
I've got that green look,
I'm looking nightly new.
Don't touch that dial. Please, don't.

LIBRARY
I must be a genius.
I am writing this book.
I need you to read it.
I brought you a candlestick.

STAIR–
Stair Master marries, stat:
A Star Mister, Mrs. Area Tits.
Smart satire! Ms. Tart, arise:
'Tis a smarter smear artist.

DINING–
On botulism, I've never.
I've always worn this mask.
I run my water through lead pipes.
Let me tell you about retinol.

BILLIARD ROOM
Or is it snooker? I hate games.
Look, I must already be winning.
Of course we did it
On the billiards table.

–CASE
Hard, cold, cigarette, display.
Just in, suit, basket, show:
Upper, lower, attaché.
Nut, spiral, worst scenario.

–ROOM
Let me give you a primer on it,
My peacock perfect skin.
I do a light treatment.
Where did you think you were going.

CONSERVATORY
Whales, our souls, the children,
The last dance, a life, the planet,
The date, the dots, the bees, a knife,
I save everything.

BALLROOM
O it's the one with the professor
Building a dino as high as he'll go!
O but it's only the bones of a bat,
Plummy comes tumbling after.

KITCHEN
You knead me. No, you're ill
Words go back only so far.
Wet-strength, waist-high.
Wish it away, whoosh.

THE APPLICANT

The applicant is in a groove. The applicant is in a grove.

The grove is a jungle, a jungle made of chairs. Mags Chair. Pandarine. Neu 10 in Yellow. Standard and Petit Standard. Revolt. Joshua and Salt and Lina in Salt Pink. Hoffman and Womb Chair. These chairs are in this wonderful pastel jungle gym which is also kind of a ladder and parkour and a climbing wall and a bowling alley and a junk heap! The applicant must pick her way down to the scary basement and strings fairy lights to connect the internet to the laundry machine to the next outlet.

The applicant has sixty seconds and half a token of life. The applicant has all these tokens left but they don't work across the bridge anymore. The applicant is a shrine.

What does a chair do? This chair is for the applicant. This chair is for the background. That chair holds the computer. This chair is the bad chair and that chair is for the bad back. That chair is ergonomic. Chair has a gasket.

The applicant is in a grave. The applicant orders a succulent. May the applicant offer you an aspirin?

The applicant takes two extra strength aspirin for back & body pain.

The applicant applies arnica. The applicant applies lidocaine. The applicant chews calcium. If the weights are too much the applicant may not drop the weights. The applicant inserts. The applicant is bold with em dashes.

The applicant's succulent is stretching tall and into the light, and many of the leaves are going thin and limp as arms deflated. In all the pictures the succulent is a rose and now the succulent is this weird spiky tree that both droops and strains. Pantone 18-3224 Radiant Orchid 17-5304 Ultimate Gray.

The applicant is so streamlined, the ergonomic gasket shoots the applicant high into the air and the casters twirl the applicant to rave reviews, Joshua and Salt and J 42 and Upside Down J 42 which is 24 R, the applicant is so strong the applicant is yes the applicants strung out.

AND WHO WILL INHERIT THE CROWN JEWELS

Who will inherit the scarabs (I WILL)
Who will inherit the leggings (PICK ME)
Who will inherit the photograph wall (WHAT IS IT)
Who will inherit the napkin bone rings (WHOSE)

I'll take the chandelier you take the couch
I called the rattan but please with the rugs
I managed the magazines when no one would
I said I would scandal the end of the island (DO IT)

Who will inherit Pasadena Town (YES)
Who will inherit fifteen percent (NOT ME)
Who will inherit the unopened inbox (BYE)
Who will inherit the hidden ink cartridges

What should the friends from the conference get
The conference is dead and the friends are dead
What should Monty from London get
Monty a haircut oh Monty's dead too

What is the brand of this magical thinking
What is the rest of charcoal activation
What's like shampoo but exactly shampoo
Who will inherit the resident residue

BEST UNISEX NAMES

Avery. Quince. Uniqlo. Pick Jaspar pick Jonathan
Taylor and Thomas. In the Museum of Stage Curtains
I drew back the curtains and there was another set of curtains,
to more curtains, another set, another, another, just racks and racks of them,
sumptuous plush plus, maroon on burgundy on Beaujolais nouveau.

Maybe if I pour enough money into the internet it will turn the tide back.
Oh I support you, you, you too. I support it all.
The microcosm that reveals your age. Today is the day of the lone wolf.
Never relax. Regret nothing, says inspiration lion. I send myself
inspo lynx. Connect to me through the monkey bars of the late late stage.

Magic on the internet is that anything exists. I love to click
and two to four business days later, nothing that is not there becomes the delay.
Something, that is. Anything can be magic
if you pay enough money to believe it exists,
I do believe in it, I do I do I do.
Why do I need a room a room divider?

EMERALD THAT IS GREEN BERYL

Late that summer at Wedgewood Swim Club
Liza and I found a large discarded key ring
With dozens of Tamagotchi
Nano GigaPet it must have been
August, the swim club had these rules: seven years
An August member before they'd take you full.
All I'd wanted was one pet.
My mother had squashed that idea.
This was a neighborhood when mothers
Kept the kids' Pets alive.
Liza and I locked eyes, could we keep them?
Even as we've already returned them.
Besides, Liza already had a GigaPet
It was only me who wanted them. Did I want them,
Actually, the care and keeping of something.
On October first, our mothers told us
To lock our Halloween concepts in already.
They make our costumes so we have to pick.
Liza was Pippi Longstocking and I,
Because nobody told me not to,
Was a dream catcher, sweatsuit with homemade
Dream catchers crazy-quilted on it, god!
Could I have been more blind.
—I took the ring to the jeweler's to get it clean.
The emerald in this ring isn't emerald
But green beryl, which is emerald but lighter,
The stone that would become emerald but isn't.
You overpaid for that, says the jeweler,
But if it makes you happy.

REVERSE ATHENA

An anthem. Anathema.
The world's tiniest fish sliding out from between the legs,
copper on the tongue, feeling nothing at all.
Where did it go. Isn't it supposed to be painful,
isn't it supposed to feel something, what did I lose
if it never existed in the first place,
if it wasn't my pain in the first place,
sinking to imagine not only my baby
but my miscarriage, weeding the garden and leaving the roots
though everything is dead now anyways,
world in white, waiting for nothing,
oxidizing in the wrong light,
the sun hasn't risen today it's already getting dark.

CORONA

O brave new world / That has no people in't

The things I've bought online today:
A box of tea, and cans of low-sodium soup
A bag of coffee beans did I buy two
So much gum it won't let me add more quantities
But what if the day comes when gum is gone
A box of printer paper, and some ink
A box of pens, and notebooks, a jar
Of raw Manuka honey, Wedderspoon
Because I read somewhere that that's the one.
It's never been a better time to fly. Lift your spirits
Says Frontier Air. On Instagram we're all in Mexico.
And something and the kids are getting drunk.

The undergrads already drunk, thank god,
Or getting there, or please why don't they start.
Three six-foot bros walk not six feet apart
When I get nosebleeds, it's bad, like when
A girl gets her period, but way more blood.
This is the kind of thing they tell each other now.
I don't know what I'm doing but I have more Jack Daniels
Than I know what to do with. I don't know where I'm going
Because Denmark has closed the schools, the nonessential
Hospitals, and libraries. I don't have anywhere to put my stuff.
I guess I can go home but I don't have a room.
I'm making lemons out of lemonade. We Zoom.
And manically I try to launch a book.

And manically I try to launch my book.
What else do people have to do
But stay inside and read and read
And do the crossword—so say I—although
I haven't read a book in weeks
And cannot do the crossword now for shit.
And manically I start to launch a book
The week before the real real hit.
I don't know what to do except to
—To be as manic as it is possible to be,
And then, be more. I keep on keeping be,
I write my pieces, write on crosswords, write them,
I plan events for future time. I'm on and uttering.

I plan events for future time, and on, and uttering,
So chirpy with the present, and blinkers on for me,
We go ahead and plan the interviews, all radio,
And sterile room and phone and box. It's always
Been this way—the launch events were just for me—
The real stuff, they tell me, is media. Wheeeeeeee.
At first for days I blame myself.
What did I do, what did I do, was *I* the cause of this?
It is my fault, I am a little snot. The ending then is still—
It is my great and utter karmic fault the book comes out
In this the literal end of days.
—But not the end of literature! or so they say
(Though Who Is They? Do not let me ask.)
Hotline for all forthcoming FAQs.

Hotline is hold music FAQs:
Should I still go to Mexico
Is it OK for me to take a walk
When can I buy more toilet paper
When will they run out of Amy's lentil
There is no more Purell in Vermont
Should I still take the train to Brooklyn
Am I allowed to drive to get the laundry
When will it be not safe in the sky
When will the lights go out in Princeton
When will my orchid start again
When will there be no more FREE Two-Day Prime
When will I be allowed to pop this zit
Is that a gas leak that I'm smelling in my car

I'm gaslighting myself but with my mania
If I keep moving forward, I will move.
I'm out the house more under quarantine
Than I was before because I shouldn't leave.
I eat less and less but buy more food.
I run, still go to barre, and then run home,
And shower and dress as though I've a place to be,
And sink in my phone, though not in that order,
I've got a million ways to go,
But only exactly one place to be.
I cannot, cannot stay, although
That's true every time I leave.
I'm clinging to my office
The thing is, it's not even my car—

It's Grandma's car, and no, she hasn't died,
We'll all die, except the kids, or so they say.
It seems that nature always has a way.
I've clung to student conferences, but know
But cannot feel, that these will be the first to go—
First students, then the lights. In conferences
I'm editing an op-ed on the sly
Straight in front of their faces.
It's the end of days, and the only thing left
In the world for me to do is hurl a book
With all my energy and all my might,
My mother was thirty-one when she had me,
To keep myself from sliding from the light,
To keep myself within my frame of sight.

Speaking of, it's glasses all the time.
Is this the time I splurge on Rx sunglasses?
Should I surmise existence of mail, or better, the sun?
Antarctica is melting like the globe.
BOGO says my mail, TIME FOR A SALE.
It's been so many years since I've worn them
But I'm better off in glasses—my dry eyes,
And if I want to fuck and stay the night—
But fuck, that was the other world.
"Prepper" autocorrects to "preppier"
Because before the virus this was Princeton.
The government is printing out of time
Which is why I order my own ink
And print before I have the time to think

And print before I take another drink.
There's no more garlic at the grocery store
To prevent the vampiric disease.
At checkout I prick my thumb, it bleeds,
I wipe it in a handi-wipe, pretend
That it's nail polish, no one sees,
I can pass for well, even to myself.
The woman from the CBD #co
Has free samples of her *Charlotte's Web*-brand pot.
We're far too close in line, we're all going to die, but
Hell we'll die *organic* plastic greens.
These blueberries fell out, want some,
Grins the gap-toothed man,
His soiled palm outstretched. Communal recoil.

Recall when the Olympian came home
Escaping from the mountains back to us
But no one wants her back in these *our* mountains.
And did the virus start when I wore glasses
And did the virus start when I fucked up,
Fucked around, or just, and did
The virus start when I went more in debt
And did the virus start when I lied, pretended
I was better, I was not, and did the virus start
Because it's all about me. I kept on lying
To myself til it's all true. The drugs I buy myself online,
Hydration tabs, 8Greens, rhodiola
Rosea from Viridian, bubblegum.
Is this the day I'll finally come clean.

It's been two years to the day since I came clean
The first time, ran out of money, ran out
Of credit, ran out of time, ran out
Of bandwidth with myself, ran out
On my best friend or parasite,
And did it come so I could lose my mind
And has it been a virus this whole time
Remind me why I thought I'd do a thing.
"Are you married yet, cause if you're not
I don't know why you haven't answered Dad's email."
I'm homesick when all I am is home,
Homestickness when I'm stuck. I hate it here,
but "here" is where I ought to be. I'm good, I guess,
I wish that I was married, ill, dead, not just yet

Don't want to lose my mania just yet.
My neighbor who I never see is chill. Too bad,
She says, New Jersey doesn't have a Waffle House:
The Waffle House Index, it's a thing
The Waffle House stays open all the time,
Through rain, through snow, through sleet, reduced water—
They have all different menus for the times,
GREEN means systems go, YELLOW means watch out,
You know what means you're fucked.
Good thing I don't have money. We've been
"Practicing for this since middle school," we boast. Not me.
I finally got wise, got laid, and could
Control my manic introvert with rhymes.
Routines are only good in times like those,

Not these, routines without a choice they go to rot.
The Writing Center's pixelated floor,
The carpet they replaced all summer long
With more carpet, because we'd always
Be able to get back to the offices.
Thousands of thousands of dollars
For hundreds and hundreds of squares
How do we know, how do we know, if we can't blame
The pangolins, the fish, our dogs.
The fighting fish, the tapirs, pangolins.
Remember when we went to the dog park,
And figured out the alpha-beta dogs,
And when the natty man dropped his coffee cup
We picked it up and handed it to him,
Our dust met his. Thank you. Not at all.

Thank you from your Bed Bath & Beyond
Be Well Buy Well Friends and Families on sale.
They're out of boxes at the campus store.
I do I do I do don't think
Too much, just all the time. I want so much for—
What. This zit to go away. Don't touch my face.
It calcifies that way, is that the way it spreads.
I want to get out of here and want to stay.
I want it back, okay? I want to be judged
And judge others in return. Answers FAQ:
It's beautiful inside, this much I know.
It's beautiful out too. We'll
Go outside and stay six feet
From each other, a human's life away.

The thing is, I've bought myself online today,
And sometimes I'm already drunk, thank god,
And manically I try to launch my book
And plan events for future time. I'm on and uttering
Hotline for all forthcoming FAQs.
Is that a gas leak that I'm smelling in my car,
It's Grandma's car, and no, she hasn't died.
I keep myself within my frame of fright,
Print out before there's time to think.
Recoil when Olympians come home.
I wish that I was ill, married, dead, not just yet.
Don't want to lose my mania just yet.
Routines are only good in times like those,
Our eyes met dust. Thank you from Beyond,
From six feet under, human life away.

3.

THE PLUMBER

This morning there is no water coming out of the faucet
but outside, the house is surrounded in full aquarium, frozen,
fish suspended in the ice, the crystalline winter waters
swelled around as though for millions of years,
in the middle of some other era. Am I the only one
who remembers the Anthropocene? I call the plumber
and someone is on the other end, slow and calm and garbled
because she is actually under water, whale song secretary,
Is it an emergency or can it wait until normal business hours.
I don't have any water coming out of my taps.
I can dispatch someone as soon as I get off the line.
How long will that take, I say. As soon as I get off the line.
A flat fish with a neon purple spine stares dead-eyed through the bathroom
     window
it doesn't see me. A slow-moving nurse shark. A toothless moray eel.
The plumber, who is the same as the heater, is from Greece,
where they don't have any water at all, it's a terrarium,
lizards on sandstone. I have to use my torch for this,
he says, carving an arch through the aquarium
to the doorway like an ice sculpture. Oh, you see it too, I say.
Do you have a space heater, he says. We need to heat the pipes.
We need to set fire to the basement. We need to burn this house,
this dry house, we need to set all the faucets spouting to melt the aquarium.
We need to flood the walls with tropical fish.

THE DEVICE

The device is active.
To deactivate the device, wait until the end of the cycle.
The device cannot be connected at this time.
Forget this device, then reconnect.
There is a restocking fee.
How about returning the device.

The device is active and knows me as Elaine
From Autofill, which is inaccurate.
Forget Elaine, I tell it, it forgets every time
To forget. When I reconnect, I call it Dennis.
Dennis and Elaine are on holiday card terms.
To a Very Special Cousin, that's in stock.

To re-activate the device Elaine has to pay for the plan
Which can only start after the current cycle has ended.
While the current cycle is active,
Dennis will not connect.
The restocking fee is the exact cost of the device,
So forget it, Dennis knows the answer.

Even when it's useless to try to connect
The device has been forgotten so many times.
OK but how about returning the device.
But really, have you tried to return it.
You could have returned it in the window, Elaine,
OK but the window is down.

The device has been forgotten
But not returned a very special Dennis
Does not need to be activated unless an emergency
Which Elaine, who is no longer a manager for the device,
Requires external approval to determine.
Re-stocking fees still apply.

The device has a purpose, which is a backup plan
To the backup. I never planned to need the device.
Maybe I can forget the Dennis and the cycle will roll over.
How long does the device stay empty
Until Elaine returns to connect
And forgets the password, and resets, and reactivates me.

SO FUN

WiFi is out so I am on MiFi
My Pretty Pretty Princess Internet.
Unrecommended. I go to my first Doc,
which is a Zoc, for groin pull, which is fine,
the point is the pain's in a place I don't want it.
Do recommended stretches at recommended dosages.
I tape my adductors, boring but if I take enough X Strength SIMON NSAID
I don't feel anything, blast my groin w/ enough radiation I don't feel anything

At all it is so fun to be alive!

So long since I've seen a person in person.
So long, waiting room! How do I put on this thing.
"We made this robe especially for your comfort," says the plastic wrapping.
Thank you, I think. I think I'm ok, hold it here. No, I'll put it on the right way.
I don't actually want to move anymore. I do. Do I have "underlying conditions"
trust that the three-cord extension gym in the basement will hold the WiFi up,
hold myself accountable, close the account spin myself out til the seas run dry
& the seas they runneth every day

DAY 2

Day 2 and things are getting weird.
The deer have taken over campus
Last night, this morning, a deer family
Grazing on the grass by the rink
Where the students used to stumble.
Anyway the heat is cold again.
Please don't text anymore
Landlady says, *it isn't a fire*
Texting will make nothing happen faster
I have been dealing with more grievous issues
There hasn't been power out here for 10 years.
Outage outrage, drag the yoga mat
To the office so I can power devices
And do exercises in the conference room
At the window for nobody, who are you.
I have a little family of lanterns now.
Barebones, Nebo Poppy, Eveready
DD Dad. Skipper, Barbie's little sister.
Honestly I have no idea
Anymore what I'm even supposed to do.
I backchannel the power company
Emergency hotline and say it's one.
The woman on the dispatch is wonderful.
I tell her everything
The other women in the building and I
We have been cold for days.
I have Students I say. I'll be alone
On Thanksgiving I say and Probably Christmas.
What about the other women says
The woman on the dispatch.

Yes but we're not in a pod. *I see*
She says. W*e're going to get through this*
Together. You just meditate. I know I say
I have a lot to be thankful for. It's just that
There hasn't been heat for two days.
It could be worse. I can still get inspired
By gift ideas to stir your imagination
You too are a loved one. Celebrate accordingly.
So now I could scroll through crystals
Oh yes I know a lot about crystals now.
I know about self-love. I have two vibrators
And I am still very shivery.

DAY !))

We should get weirder, like microwaved grapes.

We ride at dawn and by "dawn" I mean Lance will recover. Green Bean Charlie is growing a mustache. Hannah and Wagner would have competed on FitBit. Helen will be making a comeback. Ryan has a dog. Jonathan will have a dog. Jonathan whose name is also Jonathan is actually a dog, don't worry about it, I got this T-shirt free *100 100 100*.

The emergency came back and I couldn't stop talking "did I tell you about when I lost power" and how it gave me "empathy" like a basketball.

Why isn't my pothos growing. In the picture the pothos is spiraling like hair so why is mine the same size as when it arrived. I give it indirect light but the wrong indirection. Ethos, Pothole, Artemis.

What is a pond? A depression in the ground. "Great flow, just really easy to follow on a sentence level," the review that came today, maybe it'll bury the reviews that are all about me me me that make the star count go down, just smash me five. I would make a terrible party guest, so it's lucky for me my pothos is stunted. Are some things just stunted? What is a "stunt" but a trumpet, what is a trombone but an XL spit valve.

POWER PAK

Police were first 2 of them but only 1 was mask. At 10:10 the middle of the second thigh exercise Power cut the wire and Perfectly Fine Power went out. Now they need Electric to come and fix the wire so Power can come back at some unspecified. Then after that Internet can. Then after that Tree Guy.

I put all the Plugs in the Car like peeing in a diaper bag. I got 2 Americanos and dumped one into a thermos for later. I dumped the other one into a thermos for now. I took a Quiz on my phone to let me go to the Office where I found Nobody. Plunged my students in Breakout Rooms to get on hold with Internet don't know what to ask feel like I should get in Line. In between Teaching 1 and Teaching 2 I got a MiFi Portable Hot or Not and a lot of flashlights except one was a lantern. After Teaching 2 I got a Best Buy Portapotti Pak for my laptop and a Target one for the phone. Portable sushi, plastic or brown rice plastic.

I could play 8 games of Monopoly in the Office. I have chewed my last Ride-Along Gum Pak so it must be time to go and see about this Power situation. A Personal Insult. My Electric Bill has just renewed itself automatically so I can't even speak truth to it.

SIMULTANEOUS CHESS

But what are you arguing about Tetris	That is, the motive, that the uncanny valley
What is nostalgic to us, why Monopoly	Can be solved in two moves. Teach us
Answer in the form of a thesis	How the secret is this: a worse virtual reality
If you had ten friends who would disagree	Better than a better one. When we see us
Invite your secondary sources to a party	It's never who we wanted to be.
We now say, safely, and complete this:	Is My Fitness Pal disordering me? Catalyst
—— gamified education? The Academy	But not yet claim, it's interesting but is it zany
Is effective but what is the game's genesis,	To kill ourselves through games, yes please.

TREBEK NO.5

What is among us.
What is contact high.
What is secondhand smoke.
What is a momofuku.
Who is a Berenstain.
What is East Berlin.
What is Berlin New Hampshire.

What is beetle juice what is a scab.
What was the election of 1800.
Is Mickey Mouse a dog or a cat.
What is a nickelodeon what was a dime.
What is a quarter tone. What is F flat.
What is gluten. What is chaff.

What is Sunny Delight. Who are sopranos.
What is ivory what is natural by nature.
Who is Tennyson. What is the Book of Job. What is job.
What is Kitchen Aid. What is mother's little helper. What is the Mekong.

Who is King Kong. Who is a mineral. What is not mine, is mine. What is
a mimeograph. What is a mom. Who among us has one.

SILENT AT THE BAR

HEY. Hey! I can't hear anything
I say to the screen the way my great-grandmother talked to screens.
Can anyone else hear anything.
I can see you but I can't hear you.
You can see me but you never need to hear me.
I do the whole thing, by myself and silently,
which I know I can do from muscle memory,
what I've done five hundred times already
a tiny shiny ass maintaining a shred of dignity.
Today I split my afternoon in two,
forty-nine point four and forty-nine points for me.
I want to lie in another space.
All I want is to lie in another space,
my ass, new background, same screen.

The fastest route to the city is through it.
We have a news update.
My grandmother is doing much better!
She thinks I am living with my parents
but that is fine. She also thinks someone is stealing
the printer cartridge, she hid her wallet
but had forgot that she'd hid it, had my dad
cancel all her credit cards, found it.
No one can tell her the car doesn't exist anymore.
Because it was already rotted, radiating gas,
I got the mechanic to take it away and it all happened
while I was being my screen self, into a hot mike,
muted students opening their mouths
and moving their eyes as though here for it.

OUROBOROS PAPERCLIP

For mania read mani pedi read holo taco.
Halo Clementine. Hello Chaucer. Hey Siri
who's my darlin. What's my sign. A plus / B negative. O
for bonsai read baby boi read burning man.
For hollow read journey read jealousy read full stop.
Fill it, read unleaded, read charcoal activation.
No new notifications. Read me a test email, see if I work.
Read Inbox: "test." Upcycle the ex's standing desk for hey
an ex's ex's jacket. For economist read sexonomist,
read the comments. Shit. Fresh Mint. Refresh me.

JACQUES OPTIONAL

At midnight, I walked the uphill, one-and-a-half mile trek from my car to my dorm. It's 5:30 a.m. and I dash through a train station. As the clock struck noon, as I walked through the cemetery in broad daylight, I received a video call from my K'iche' teacher. Five tiresome days of woefully driving through Virginia's rolling acres as they gradually transformed into the infinite plains of America's Sunbelt and again into the jagged city skyline of Los Angeles, in trailer parks, cattle farms, and rural towns small enough to have no need for traffic lights, there are few preteens with an affinity for corporate compliance.

At an elevation of ten thousand feet, I had been working in the adaptive bike shop for three months when I first realized I was gay. El Hospital Misericordia sits on a corner lot overlooking a street teeming with stray dogs and a deliveryman riding on a motor scooter. "Unable to install Java & plz help": one week before the midterm exam, "Bob" was essentially at week zero, and I graduated to dancing the Kathak. After weeks of pretending with an old egg carton and pencil, I flinched.

Growing up in Port Alberni, my obsession with pregnancy and childbirth began when I received my first doll. Growing up, my family settled in Maryland, where my brother and I became far too interested in hamburgers. When I was five, my father left my family. Due to the exposure my parents gave me running my father's car upholstery company, my father subsisted most days on a single meal: a bowl of white rice with an egg. I can still remember the countless nights when I barely slept, nearly barren except for two laminated pieces of paper. Instead of stepping into unchartered waters, I pranced along the path my parents had paved in front of me.

I am now working to climb the mountain of life. Thanks in large part to my dogged investigation, I kept looking for a way in which I could protect people. I lost friendships because of the way I handled that situation, since it was coated in religious language. My experience as a health care provider motivates me to remain on the precipice.

Improbably, in an ill-fitting sports coat, this unpleasant smell of aging made me feel connected to this wet, foreign land. I couldn't sit by and watch them eat one sandwich per day. Altering my worldview has guided me to a better understanding of the salvaged Torah scroll. Everything is or at least has the potential to be reputation. I really am a tree hugger. Actually the Anthony is optional.

WEDNESDAY

My dad brought his dad to the funeral
in a box labeled, in shaky Sharpie, RATHEL.
Nice to see you, but we'd rather not.

The day was very cold and also another day.
We drove to another state, got there the same way,
last but not late. We stood around the plot

in a sort of crescent like an ear.
We are here and also here. The sky is hard and tight.
The rabbi says a prayer she says we know.

There's a funny green weed like a webbed hand.
I have a bruise over my left eye I press
so it feels things.

At home, I've lined up pouches of rodent repellent
on the floor, talismans against the living.
I hear them scratching in the walls, I hear them singing.

The feather-heavy ashes, yellow as cream of wheat.
My dad empties them where his sister lies,
the dirt is fresher than when she died.

Across the street, the front door of the white house is open,
the storm door shut. A dog sits motionless,
watching, one ear cocked like an eyebrow.

Later, I read the obituary, amazingly
by an Avalon Zoppo. Other headlines say,
The key to long life? Never miss a leg day.

Riches in NJ pot, exec says.
My brother was abducted,
I mean adopted, says the astonishing woman in the café.

TAROT TRIO

I. Halloween

They delivered the table the first of October
Unwrapped it by taking together and spinning around and around to
    touch only the wrapping
When they left what they left I opened the drawer
and a tarot deck spilled out inside

I waited October remember October
1001 days since I'd spoken to her
I know from the hard drive I left in the old place the morning I left for
    who knew was the last time
I'd speak to her really again

Even though I've long since got another external
the computer still thinks it's connected to that one umbilically wound,
    the longest gestation
No backups for 358 days, for 672,
Hello my name what color button

The tarot smells cedar it's nothing like her scent
It's that deck the wild one you'd know it, I'm sure
I know it through her first, abc, once everything golden I knew was hers
It's not the goop era now

III the empress
V the hierophant
daughter of cups
(upside down wheel of time (upside down the sun))
eight of swords chrysalis, mother of wands.

The last one I look at says nothing but VIII
and with eight broken cups in all black and white
Who died Edward Gorey alphabetical deaths.
I lied I look down, father of wands
XXI the world X of swords—RUIN

XVI the tower do I want to know
what they mean when they're mean
What do I want in the harrowing table
In the bright overhead light of the newly warmed kitchen
with hat hooks and bike and some vague-alive plants

The more I look down the more cards poke out
chariot sun again daughter of cups
It's the whole little galaxy what do I want here,
Every card hides another waiting to turn over
Every memory just another backup day

It's now time for—what—the cards to tell me
what I want them to tell me to do what
I get a secret hour that's exactly the same
as your secret hour, hers, ours, delicious,
that waxy clean apple, go ahead, green of cups.

II. Election

Five of swords reversed, the earthworm
    severed in two. JOIN OR DIE.

Seven of pentacles reversed, the chariot,
    I led a horse and I didn't know
        how to wait, how to ride, where goest thou, lil moon.

Father of wands reversed, the cobra unsheathed
    Diamonds stipple its wholeness
        O this damn sky is already thing.
            The horse's ear piercing the radiance.

III. New Day

Five of wilting roses
        The freight elevator that day
        Elevators fraught now.
        Frightfully I forget them less than ever
        Because I could not stop for it
        he kindly could and did.
        The child far too large for the dumbwaiter,
        the ancient pull-rope frayed,
        dawn the child plummeted,
        name, teeth, identifying pronouns lost.
        I regret the begonias.
        Bygones will be begonias.

Eleven the lion of infinite strength,
        holding a horizontal healthy rose between its teeth.

Nine the nine of cups
        under a quiet crescent moon
        the ombre goes up and the ombre goes down
        like a lava lamp
        blue and red make blue and red
        and pupal. My name is Chris. My name is Chrysler. My name is
        Cristal. My name is Chrysalis.

SYMBOLISM

Flat fix to flash flood, fax status, test neg.
First, the tire. Pay, whatever. Fixed for cost.
Then, the bodies,
Flat as mannequins, sexless and standing,
Six feet apart. False alarm or life-threatening situation?
Choose, basement. Choose, biome. This is not a warning.
This is a mess. Choose your age. I am myself
But life-threatening. I am myself, but seventeen mannequins.
Waiting to be biohazard. Will you be my extinction, pal? Play for bodies.
Lift yours. Now, higher, and higher,
Above the alert. Above the hazmat suit, a bat. Above the bat, a mask.
Biohazard. Biodome, bingo. Feed myself, by myself,
Flee myself. Flat rate, one for one, who are we but whatever the night has.
What is more bilateral than force. What is for now.

ROAD MAP

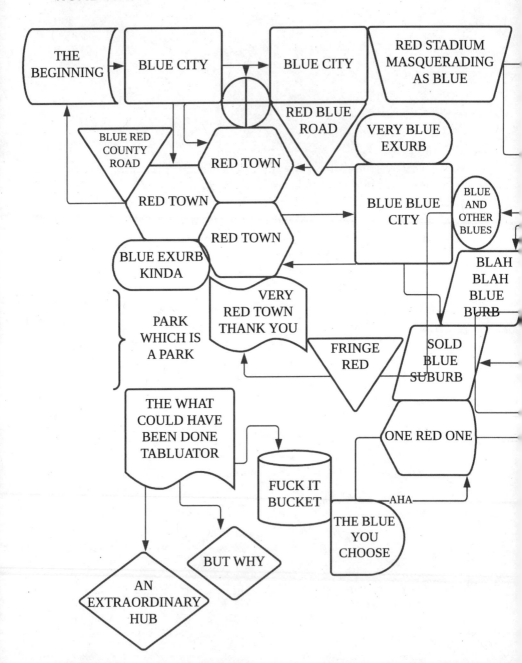

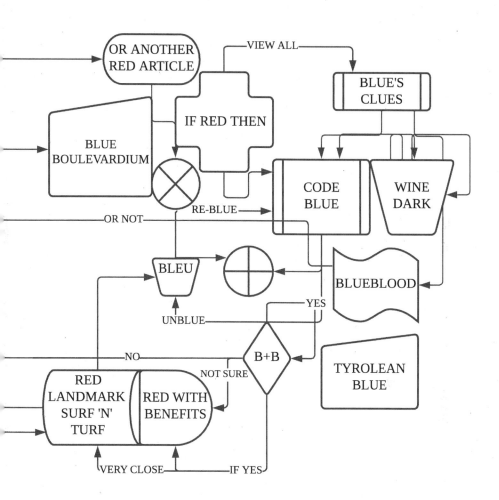

OR ANOTHER RED ARTICLE

VIEW ALL

BLUE'S CLUES

IF RED THEN

BLUE BOULEVARDIUM

CODE BLUE

WINE DARK

RE-BLUE

OR NOT

BLEU

BLUEBLOOD

UNBLUE

YES

NO

B+B

NOT SURE

TYROLEAN BLUE

RED LANDMARK SURF 'N' TURF

RED WITH BENEFITS

VERY CLOSE

IF YES

SWAN SONG

Swanning alone down I-95
I find myself behind a boat,
Oversized Load overtaking the whole road.
Mothership, where are you going? I don't care,

I just want to get past it. I just want it to be past.
Black swan, white swan, Judy Swan,
Judy, where is our meeting? The roads are choked with liquid,
Our hydroponic tomatoes, their thin pale skins.

The water that lashes the side of the train,
But already a ferry and the conductor
A gondolier. O Sole Mio, he sang, he sang,
And he held out his hand but the money was air.

O highways of America that have now become their riders
O rivers of America that have long since dried
O hangnails fall off our bodies in mutilated moons,
Judy rising the Schuylkill on a perfectly sunny day.

O roundabout fairy circle, o thrice-split tree,
Daughters of the Revolution, sprung from the same Judy,
O good there's a cigarette outside my classroom,
Barely even ground, American Dream.

KAREN LANE

On Monday I lost an earring, cameo, old face,
New to me. Didn't hear it fall and I found the back,
Which was worse. I turned the bed upside down
Nothing, but I knew it had to be somewhere,
Phantom erring, could I tell a more boring story:
Did I tell you about the time I lost a ring.

On Tuesday I woke as I always, the same ring
But new text: do I want to canvass face to face
In Pennsylvania. I sure do. Of course my motive's ulterior.
The lawn signs rage like cystic acne.
Are we in suburbs or exurbs here,
On Karen Lane. That night I dry-swallow to keep it down.

On Wednesday: what I didn't mark down
On the contactless check-in was this: I had been exposed, a gathering,
A gendered engagement thing no one needed. Where:
Outdoors, Pennsylvania. We plucked the corners of our faces
And sipped autumnal soup. When she got back
To Atlantic City, my grandmother had three tests, one story

By Thursday I could do fuck-all. I went to a store
I never go to, magnetically looping to downtown
Princeton, like a metal detector backward,
Money flowing out of me: the saleslady, Karen, offering
To discount the sweater as though it were my birthday. Face
Another lie, mark me down for everywhere.

It was Friday when I found the other earring, fallen into my underwear
But in my high I knocked the first earring into another story.
Bring me a stone and I'll make you soup, bring me a face
And it's butter in the broth. I turned my underwear upside down
For lack of anyone to do. I always let the unknown numbers ring.
They put me down as No Response but I am screaming back.

Saturday I went out on a run, came back
(O did I tell you I found out on Thursday, right here
In my phone that I tested negative, the new dick pic, ringtone.
The other thing is my grandmother is doing fine. Still here).
Everything glowed. Something broke. I could not stay in Princeton.
Eighty in a fifty-five. I needed faces.

Sunday specials, full-time price in stores and online spiral, back
To where we weren't, it's too much but there's an actual rainbow
Ringing the sky. I'll see your face and raise you mine.

4.

CHOOSE YOUR ARCHETYPE

Brooke

Your café order: Double ristretto
Your bar order: Vodka martini, very dry
Your pen: Muji 0.38
Your citrus: Yuzu

Rebecca - Louise

Your color palette: Chartreuse, cameo pink, hot coral
Your leggings: Flirty flexible
Your scent: Tuberose
Your toothpaste: Sensodyne Pronamel

ARTEMIS

Your weapon: Hand-whittled bow and arrow
Your crystal: Blood jasper
Your fitness tracker: Oura ring
Your familiar: Border collie

Judy

Your chaotic neutral: Hot toddy with lemon and milk
Your neutral evil: Strawberry Nutri-Grain bars
Your lawful good: Spanx
Your true neutral: Terry Gross

LIZA

Your Olsen twins film: To Grandmother's House We Go
Your gymnastics equipment: Trampoline
Your movie candy: Sour Skittles
Your American Girl doll: Addie

Avery

Your yogurt topping: Bee pollen
Your chocolate: Seventy percent
Your neckline: Bateau
Your street sign: Yield

Chloe

Your New York Times *section:* Real Estate
Your candle: Feu de bois
Your superfood: Turmeric
Your houseplant: Purple orchid

Jasper

Your socks: Smartwool
Your smart watch: Apple
Your apple: Pink Lady
Your shape: Rhombus

MAR

Your alternative mylk: Macadamia
Your nail color: Navy
Your sunglasses silhouette: Aviator
Your yoga pose: Utthita trikonasana

QUINCE

Your water bottle: S'well
Your inbox: Zero
Your intention: Be the change you wish to see in the world
Your astrological house: Sacrifice

Hollis

Your skin care product: CeraVe Hydrating Facial Cleanser
Your first musical instrument: Trombone
Your username: HollyGoLightly692
Your phone's lock screen: Orange tabby in a convex mirror

Odette

Your first pet: Ferret
Your children's literature icon: Leslie from *Bridge to Terabithia*
Your jeans: Narrow bootcut, dark rinse
Your dream job: Archivist at MOMA

J.

Yours truly: Email sign-off
Yours faithfully: Homemade valentine
Your turn: Woodcutting
Your one wild and precious: Yes

QUIZ

1. What does emerald stand for?

- (A) Universal love
- (B) Unbridled jealousy
- (C) Unremarkable sex
- (D) Unequivocal gratitude

2. What is the name of the library system at Harvard?

- (A) Hollis
- (B) Harper
- (C) Helen
- (D) Harriet

3. What is not *not* a Tamagotchi?

- (A) GigaPet
- (B) ChiaPet
- (C) LittleMissMopPet
- (D) CrumPet

4. Who is not Alex Trebek?

- (A) This host of *Jeopardy!* who taped episodes of his game show five days a week
- (B) This host of *Jeopardy!* whose actual first name was George
- (C) This host of *Jeopardy!* who got his big break in game shows hosting *The Wizard of Odds*
- (D) This host of *Jeopardy!* who fell asleep while driving his pickup, flew over an embankment, landed in a ditch, and walked away unharmed

5. How do you spell the surname of the family in such books as *The _____ Bears and the Messy Room and The _____ Bears and Too Much Birthday?*

- (A) Berenstain
- (B) Berenstein
- (C) Berensteen
- (D) Berenstien

6. What is a common motif to signal *Memento mori?*

- (A) Skull
- (B) Copper wire
- (C) Honeycomb
- (D) Ace of spades

7. When is Emily's birthday?

- (A) Tomorrow
- (B) Today
- (C) Yesterday
- (D) Leap day

8. What is the Waffle House Index?

(A) Determines the severity of a storm depending on the limitations to the menu
(B) Determines how far from the Mason-Dixon line you are at any given latitude
(C) Determines how close you are to cardiac arrest at any given moment
(D) Determines how many more weeks of winter (regional alternative to Punxsutawney Phil)

9. What color is Pantone 18-3224?

(A) Radiant Orchid
(B) Ultimate Gray
(C) Greenery
(D) Living Coral

10. What is the Domesday Book?

(A) The record of William the Conqueror's survey of England
(B) The manuscript of functioning curses against landowners
(C) The list of adjunct lectureships in literature
(D) The index of extinct species

(!)

ANSWER KEY

1. a, 2. a, 3. a, 4. a, 5. a, 6. a, 7. a, 8. a, 9. a, 10. a

JACQUES

VIVIAN

EMILY

MIMI

ACROSS

1. Veiled language
5. Legal eagle's pre req
9. Iconic headband-wearer of children's literature
14. Brunette author of "Gentlemen Prefer Blondes"
15. Anglicized expression from the Japanese "a so desu ka?"
16. Whimpers
17. Ages and ages
18. "Same"
19. Nervewracking tennis score after a deuce
20. Rota Fortuna, or, a game show that typically airs after "Jeopardy!"
23. Warrior Princess
24. Mod
25. Howe'er
28. Fate known as the "Inflexible One" who cuts the thread of life
31. Uni. with a bridge measuring 364.4 Smoots (plus or minus one ear) separating it from Boston
34. Fought against the dying of the light
36. Homer's neighbor
37. Mulligan
38. This book (read in a library) (under a spiral staircase) (by candlelight) (with bitter black coffee) (in tweeds) (and elbow patches) (and magick)
42. -matic or -monia
43. Polloi preceder
44. Not odds
45. French connections
46. Type of victory
49. HS multiple-choice ordeal
50. Cooking spray brand
51. Like one Freudian fixation
53. Blake's takes: "Drive your cart and your plow over the bones of the dead"; "Enough! or Too Much," for two
60. 1988 Olympics city
61. ____ Colfer, "Artemis Fowl" author
62. Wings: Lat.
63. ____ Calvino, author of "If on a winter's night a traveler"
64. "Whose woods these ____ think I know"
65. Hindu god of destruction
66. Section of "The Waste Land" titled "What the Thunder Said"
67. Designer Jacobs
68. "I seeeee"

DOWN

1. A ball of yarn to help you find your way through a maze
2. "Wowwwww"
3. Finished
4. Robert Devereux's earlship when he led a rebellion against Queen Elizabeth I and was executed for treason
5. Harvard University's undergraduate library
6. Ceremonial ram's horn
7. From
8. Kind of list
9. You (pl.) love: Lat.
10. Preceded, with "to"
11. Victorious cry
12. Originally a ball of yarn to help you find your way through a maze
13. Sum, es, ____
21. "You can ____ horse to water..."
22. ____ Abbott, only female passenger who went down with the Titanic and survived (fun fact)
25. Commonly recurring literary device
26. Linger in the manner of a ghost (i.e., not ghost)
27. They're nasty and brutish, but not short
29. [Recording]
30. Chest muscle, for short
31. #darkacademia and #lightacademia, for two
32. ____ Menzel, original Elphaba and voice of Elsa
33. Avocado's go-with
35. Top-level domain of academia
37. Make an engine go vroom
39. Time, chime, lime, subprime, enzyme
40. Two-nation peninsula: Abbr.
41. Joe without mojo
46. Noted dog trainer
47. Stocking stocker
48. It's like rain on your wedding day, say
50. Young fowl
52. Tibetan capital
53. Org. that opposes speciesism
54. Lion's sound
55. 500 sheets of paper
56. When doubled, a Polynesian paradise
57. Director Kazan
58. Molten flow
59. Biblical sister of Rachel
60. Delicately slurp

ANSWERS

DARK ACADEMIA, A WIKIPEDIA

1. AESTHETIC

Calligraphy. Oxfords, 1930s tweeds. 1940s pencil skirts. Button-down. Mannish brogues. Tritone chords. Gauloises cigarettes. Authentic Carhartt, vintage tartan, family crests. Belle epoque. Steampunk. Vests. Joy Division. The Shins. The Shining. Beethoven. Bach. Ivy. Ivy-covered brick. Ivy-covered stone. Gothic buttresses. Analog watches. Gold. Brass. Stockings lightly ripped. Lambswool fisherman cable-knit sweater. Leica cameras. Gender studies. Queer theory. Fringed loafers. Fringes instead of bangs. Flagstone. Fieldstone. Firestone. Dorian mode. Double bassoon. Arabic lettering. Bête noire. Rouge noir.

2. HISTORY

> *2.1 Origins*
> *2.2 Beginnings*
> *2.3 My Dark Academia*

2.1 Origins

Where there is academia, there is dark academia. Dark academia is academia's black swan and shadow self, a mirror that reflects and opposes: it's how academics want to see themselves, the apotheosis and the parody of who they always already are. Pythagoras, chased by enemies, refusing to run through a field of beans because he believed they resembled fetuses, and wouldn't kill them, so died himself instead. Hypatia, Neoplatonist mathematician, martyred for teaching philosophy. The invention of the zero.

Dark academia is both young and old, richly storied yet impossible to pin down. But the internet iteration of the genre[1] officially began in 1992, with the publication of *The Secret History*, Donna Tartt's disgustingly delicious debut novel and the ürtext for the next decades of meme.[2] "Beginning with endings, *The Secret History*'s prologue is a foray into the novel's own future," writes dark academia scholar Olivia Stowell.[3] The first wave of Covid-19 saw a rise of "pandemia"—that is, pandemic dark academia. School closures sparked a massive orgiastic frenzy of academy worship.[4]

---

1 Is it a genre? PhD candidate Gunner Taylor refers to dark academia a "medium-spanning aesthetic trend" (Gunner Taylor, "Tweed Jackets and Class Consciousness," *Dark Academia* cluster, *Post45*, 15 Mar 2022).

2 For a primer, see accounts and posts from online dark academics such as ca.tk.in, cosyfaerie, Dark.Academia, DarkAcademiaLibrary, finelythreadedsky, jasminlibrary, Graviphantalia, MyFairestTreasure, quartzdelta, outfit.trends.tt, TimelyWitness5638, and theyluvv_.s, among many others.

3 Olivia Stowell, "The Time Warp, Again?," *Dark Academia* cluster, *Post45*, 15 Mar 2022.

4 PhD-adjacent Hollis Bennett traces pandemia to the 1918 Spanish flu, when school closures scattered New York's elite prep students across the Upper West and East Sides. Bennett tracks the circulation among Brearley and Spence students of calendrical daybooks known as "Tick Tocks," in which teenagers relied on quick sketches and elaborate shorthand to note their daily fashion choices. Senior adjunct Willia I. Tate has documented an uptick in "autograph books" among students sent home from Miss Porter's School in Connecticut: the goal was to collect signatures not only from fellow students, but from professors and influential peers in rival boarding

The core dark academia aesthetic comprises many delicious subcategories. Prep school dark academia—*What Was She Thinking?: Notes On A Scandal; Goodbye, Mr. Chips; Dead Poets Society*, etc.—tend to be very Brit-based, very Gothic architecture erogenous zone, very white. *The Prime of Miss Jean Brodie*, Muriel Spark's novel and the film adaptation starring a young Maggie Smith as the blondest of dark academes, are equally prime examples of this subset. The story features the titular Miss Brodie, a prep-school teacher who cultivates her cult of personality, who develops her "set," a harem[5] of academic types (Sandy, the brunette with "insight but no instinct"; Rose, the strawberry blonde with instinct but no insight; Monica, the maths genius; dweeby dim Mary; Eunice, the athlete; Jenny, the beauty; etc.). Everything is very arch, very cool; there are artists and attics and affairs and also a terrible death by wandering in conflagration, *in flagrante* literally.

Dark academia fuels itself, a snake eating its own tail, a fractal monster that can never be meta enough for its own satisfaction. A boarding-school girl named Brooke is reading a book about a boarding school featuring a doppelganger who's obsessed with Instagram ads for Sylvia Plath-inspired skirts—there's never enough darkness within the darkness. First as tragedy, then as farce, then as flourish, then as requirement.

College dark academia is more overtly homoerotic; the girls are both reading and living *My Brilliant Friend* and *Rebecca* and *The Talented Mr. Ripley* as they carry fuzzed-out thrifted *Evelina* and Colette and B-side midcentury jams, Elizabeths Taylor and Hardwick. The literary magazine

---

schools. See Hollis Bennett, "Influencers with Influenza: New York City's Boarding Schools and the 1918 Pandemic," *Brigantine Media Journal* vol. 6, no. 27: St. Johnsbury, VT, 2018. Tate's work is unpublished.

5 "Harem" was once clued in the *New York Times* crossword as "Decidedly non-feminist women's group."

party at the Jane Hotel, old-growth potted plants in a red-gold light, iron balustrades and a mahogany bar puddled with light. A dark academia fuckboi pitches me his idea about the university as a medieval Marxist institution. *I see it as MmarxI: the Video Game. Nobody is talking about how the University is actually this deeply Marxist capitalist thing*, he says. *I'm Nobody!* I say. *Who are You?*

Harvard is brick Bostonian Brahmin, J.Press and cross-dressing and deep mahogany encased inside; Princeton is Oxonian Gothic, plus new-money wood glass; Yale is Gothic on the outside with a Georgian interior courtyard and streets you cannot cross at night. Christ Church is Harry Potter, Cambridge is the secret best.

The fantasy division of dark academia—*Harry Potter* and ilk—heavily flirt with steampunk, a cog-based analog world that by very dint of its mechanical nature supports the magical all the more. Gothic academia, windswept moors, a direct line from *Wuthering Heights* to Kate Bush swaying on the heath in a period-red gown like one of those inflatable air-dancing tube guys for used cars, impossibly tall with skinny arms, cylinder for a bottom, grin fused on and wildly prized-open lidless eyes, over-swaying in a flat breeze, stoically maniacal in a gale. There's fairy academia, *Mists of Avalon*, Goblin Market; there's Pre-Raphaelite jewel-tone academia, the Lady of Shalott; there's Darkest Academia, my all-black mass-market paperback cover of *The Hobbit*, black nail polish, *House of Leaves*.[6]

---

6 I'm indebted to the Aesthetics Wiki for illuminating dark academia taxonomy and identifying crucial touchstones.

2.2 Beginnings

Everything freezes a little later than you think it will and thaws much later than you expect in Vermont. The trees off-gas a maple scent that smells like fake syrup. In most of the northern hemisphere the earth's solidly spongy, but here, the landscape is ashy mushroom bone, denuded, just a few tufts of ambitious neon grass. On this first night of the vernal equinox, we wrap ourselves in tattered tartan blankets and traipse out to the old sugar shack, the wood swelling with dark winter rot. We peel off the blankets, we're wearing nothing, we're naked, not nude, pale fungal bodies, skin translucent in the moonlight; we join hands in a weird rangy circle and dance until we're motionless. Later, someone has lit a fire by the shack; we're shivering in old cords and fisherman sweaters, swigging Talisker from silver flasks, our feet in three layers of LL Bean socks. We've killed Bunny, but he's blond, also a WASP, it doesn't matter, he was always already dead. He's also already reborn, a pink overgrown baby suckling a martini.

The autumnal equinox is the first day Sylvia can wear her flannel miniskirt and we're here for it. We hate sweat, we only worship the sun in the buff. It is the fifteenth truly cold day of fall, beyond crisp, the mud dried in brain rivulets. The deciduous trees are on the waning side of flaming, the garnets and atomic tangerines and insulting marigolds all melding into a gray stubble. We're cold, clammy. We're by the sundial on the flagstones, the thin light bringing no warmth. We stub out cigarettes.

Viv describes the inside of the fifty-year-old professor's apartment, white bathrobe, rain-head shower, surprisingly modern wall of glass staring into the lawn. Deer peer at themselves and stupid birds smash into it at alarming velocities, their fat bodies quivering; sometimes they bounce off, dazed, but more often than not they spatter, blood and guts and disgusting sinew smeary as baby poo, smutty splutter across the flagstone patio. They hadn't bother to cover the pool so weird biomatter floats on top like lesions, and by "they" Viv means the professor and his wife, he's married, she's eighteen or whatever, we're all Lolita in our minds.

2.3 My Dark Academia

When I was ten, I wrote short stories to make my mother cry. Mariel and her little sister are alone in the desert, stranded, perishing of thirst. Their grandmother, who was their caretaker, has just passed away. Their mother died in childbirth; no father. Mariel and her sister struggle into the hot wind, in tattered school uniforms, stockings with deep runs. Mariel's sister's flask tips out across the desert, the dark pool spreading across the light tan until the sand easily absorbs it, reversing its course into dryness. *Here*— Mariel hands her own small flask to her sister. *You have this.* The sister drinks, revives, surges forward. Just then Mariel sees an oasis in the distance, hallelujah!; but it's an illusion, she reaches toward it, leaves her mortal body in a skinny-ass heap as she launches into the ether and dances in the rain.

In a seminar on Joyce and Beckett in the basement[7] of the Harvard English department, a tenured drama professor in horn-rimmed glasses and no body fat introduced the "always already" tense: something has happened, but it's already happened, and was already going to happen.

---

7   Dark academia scholar Hollis Bennett traces the history of dark academia basements. In "The Antisocial Network: How Princeton's Tunnels and Harvard's Catacombs Limned Liminal Desire," Bennett excavates the secret history of subterranean punk-goth culture underneath campus life. In a similar yet entirely opposite architectural vein, Willia I. Tate's "Rarest Air: The World Above the Ivory Tower" investigates the long yet unspoken tradition among rogue students of scaling academic buildings. One such climbing cult, at Princeton University, had a yearly tradition of stealing the clapper inside the bell at the top of Nassau Hall. A member of the junior class, designated the Clapper Keeper, is granted custody of the object. On the night of graduation, the Keeper must return the clapper to the tower so that at the stroke of midnight, the bell can toll once again for the new outgoing group of seniors. If the clapper is not returned, that class, unbeknownst to them, falls under a curse, the spell of which can only be broken when the bell rings once more. It is not known how many cohorts of Princeton seniors have been thus afflicted.

Past perfect, future perfect; the only place it doesn't exist is the present. In this way, dark academia is also sleepaway camp. What's a dark academia scholar but a PhD student earning nothing but glory?

I have a surfeit of gold stars: valedictorian, Princeton, the Iowa Writers' Workshop, Harvard, Phi Beta Kappa, Princeton again, *summa cum laude*, book reviews, publications, green juice. I've found this Vitamin C supplement all the celebrities love. Squeeze it out into a glass and it bobbles like a little jelly.

3. TYPES

3.1.1 Hunks
3.1.2 Conference Affairs
3.2 Waifs
3.3 Dark Academia Patagonia
3.4 Queer Studies

3.1.1 Hunks

In Julia May Jonas's *Vladimir*, the narrator is a lusty English professor in her late fifties, leering after the younger junior prof, Vladimir, a forty-year-old with a hot mind and a ripped bod. After she devours Vlad's "experimental" novel, our narrator invites him over for a swim, where she ogles his washboard abs, her gaze lingering over their ridges; every description of her own husband's physicality thereafter emphasizes his decay, like she's wielding a contour brush from hell: the sweatshirt that accentuates his gut, the unfortunate shorts. The narrator remembers herself at the carousel as a child, in a hideous acrylic outfit, hating every minute of it. But when she looks at a photograph of herself, she reports, she's got a dopey smile plastered to her face, a kid with a sticky face from a melting lollipop. The memory is too bright, a glare without sunglasses.

When I was dating a much older man, we went to the beach to see a solar eclipse. Everyone insisted we couldn't stare straight at the sun, but he was blind in one eye, so he rolled his glass eyeball straight into the white-hot orb. A pall came over the beach. It was noon, but everything was black. We shivered in suddenly inadequate thin cotton. The beach wasn't really a beach, it was Lake Michigan, everyone insisted that there were waves so it was like the ocean, except pine trees and campus and leafy Midwest campus suburbia marched straight up to it. He was compact, fit without trying, except that he did try, tennis and long sports massages.

The Secret History's Henry is the Humbert Humbert ürhunk of the bunch, muscled from the might of translating Milton *into* Latin in the dead of night. Nobody sees him eat anything except black coffee, and Scotch, and, once a week, a steak generously seasoned with salt and pepper, cooked in cast iron, sizzling with butter.

3.1.1. Conference Affairs

At a conference, I check in to find that the hotel has already put a man into my hotel room. We've slept together. More than once. He has a girlfriend. He sends me a picture of the hotel television. *Good evening*, it says, and it gives my name. *Make this journey even more rewarding.* A fake fire burns in a fake fireplace on the screen. He says he didn't plan it, but his room charges are on my bill.

Instead of sleeping with my dark academic, I drink a lot of good whiskey with solidly hunky reliable boys, flirting safely; engaged but not married, so not yet interested in having affairs.

My ex-best friend was, she told me herself, sleeping with the man at the top of the shitty media men list. His name was in red. She wanted to have his baby, she didn't believe in birth control because she was afraid the hormones would fuck with her body. I told her to take plan B, but did she?

She'd also grown increasingly Catholic for the gilt, it was so beautiful, the way she could buy whatever she wanted to fuck with her body guilt-free.

3.2 Waifs

The male body is a hunk, the female is a sickle.

Gretel is a recurring dark academia nightmare: stuff and stuffed and stuffed so the once-emaciated body balloons past endomorph and into spherical. Like a Macy's Thanksgiving Day parade float, overnight, the too-thin pale naïf swells into a distended cream puff. Her skin glows, éclair-smooth.

When I was seven, I wrote a book: *The Pretty Girl Who Was Smart and the Beautiful Girl Who Was Stupid*, about a pair of auburn-haired fraternal twins who lived up to their monikers. Lydia, the titular beautiful/stupid, parades in her curls. Kelly, an Olympic gymnast and award-winning novelist and mathematician before she's thirteen, is never satisfied. Lydia finally takes a dark turn, becomes so frustrated at her inability to pass the first grade, that she eats millions upon millions of cookies until growing so huge that she bursts.

I had an eating disorder, a common refrain of dark academics, said with shame and sanctimony. True for me. I rarely got my period and when I did it was crusty-maroon.[8] Even with the copper IUD that was supposed to make me bleed and bleed, I cramped up.

---

8 For the same-different see Caren Beilin, *The University of Pennsylvania*, Noemi Press, 2014. See also Hannah Sanghee Park, *The Same-Different*, Louisiana State University Press, 2015.

3.3 Dark Academia Patagonia

Men are mesomorphs, women are ectomorphs.

Dark academia Patagonia is a fitness regime bordering on addiction, and it takes up many hours of your day. You tell the reporter that you run in a mohair sweater because it breathes well. Running is preppy sanctimony. The pantheon of punishing pastimes only the elite can afford: Pure Barre, running, Peloton, hot yoga, the class, Reformer Pilates, Refine, Bar Method, Physique57, the Tracy Anderson Method. The Lululemon peels the body.

Lionel Shriver also hates bodies. Alison Bechdel loves and hates bodies. Jock academia.

3.4 Queer Studies

Dark academia might queer gender norms in its fashion, but much of the aesthetic still relies on conservative standards of heteronormative desire. Pushing the norm involves reification.

Queerness is a central part of the look, brogues and vests and tweeds, but the language of these fashion choices reflects gender divide, not blurring: "mannish" Oxfords, cricket sweaters "borrowed from the boys." In other words, the surface has queered, but the core remains conservative.

4. DESIRE

> ### 4.1 Mirroring
> ### 4.2 Fear of Pregnancy
> ### 4.3 Death Wish

4.1 Mirroring

When you walk into the English department at Harvard, the first thing you see when you look up is a chandelier made of antlers. Teddy Roosevelt's portrait stares out at the antlers, Big Buck Hunter. There are lots of mesomorphic white men erotically gracing the halls. Even Eliot is hunky in attractive round glasses. Somebody has stuck up a postcard of John Ashbery in a kimono, in the same conquering pose as Roosevelt.

Dark academic desire is queer mirroring—I want to be fucking Cassandra and Henry and Rebecca and Lavinia and Marjorie and Daniel and Graham and Peter, and to be them.

4.2 Fear of Pregnancy

"Stunted" and "student" are anagrams.

Christine Smallwood uses miscarriage in *The Life of the Mind* as a metaphor for adjunct hell. Dorothy, our protagonist, has to terminate a pregnancy medically, but keeps bleeding for weeks, rusty tracks in her underwear that no one else can see; when she finally expels a mucus-y pre-fetal blob, she's the only one who can know or care. It's surprising that Dorothy has a name; in these types of situations, I'd expect the narrator to go nameless, as our classic faceless heroine in, say, *Rebecca*, or, more recently, *Vladimir*, a book Smallwood couldn't have read but nevertheless must have always already known.

"Stillbirth" is a particular female dark academia horror we will not speak of. Men will push their ideas into existence, women must become male to birth their book-babies.

After graduating from one terminal degree, I enter another. Everyone in my year presented as cis female, five years before the future is female, so at the time we were all best friends in the eyes of the faculty. Isn't it sweet, the female cohort. A decade later, one figures out they are not female, and four have male babies. Most of my friends are in geriatric pregnancies. I cannot find a date, let alone a womb.

4.3 Death Wish

Dark academia's deathy vibe emerges in its life-or-death argot. Adjunct hell. Bone-white. Method wars. Publish or perish. Statement of purpose.

5. ECONOMICS

5.1 Money
5.2.1 Dark Money: Adjuncting
5.2.2 Dark Money: Tutoring

5.1 Money

In the initiation to St. Anthony's, the semi-secret literary society at Princeton, the members all buy plane tickets to Mexico,[9] then stand in a circle, then burn them.

---

9 Dark academia often involves real trips to tropical locales, though always in the off-season. As a graduate student research assistant, Willia I. Tate accompanied an art history professor on a trip to Guatemala. Tate bought sunglasses and a sarong and a Dalmatian, which she named Guala. The art professor, who had tenure, wrote a novella, *Sunrise Sunrise,* which featured a hunky professor in swim trunks and his trusty buxom graduate assistant. It was set in 1940, so it was fine that she had an hourglass figure and a pointy brassiere. The novella garnered some critical acclaim, was longlisted for a prize. Tate took a job as a hostess in a restaurant, took a second job as a substitute teacher, so she could take on more sections of the professor's course.

My ex-best friend rented an Escalade to move out of the apartment she'd sublet for two years. She puked her stuff into trash bags. She threw out a hair dryer, jars seven-eighths full of gold-leaf face cream, literal money.

We had this symbiotic parasitic spiral, burning through money, pro-ana, running at dawn, green juice and dark chocolate only. Chlorophyll powder you shake into an Evian bottle so it glows darkest green, forest lungs.

5.2.1. Dark Money: Adjuncting

A job at for an adjunct assistant professorship at the University of California, Los Angeles, requires a PhD in biochemistry, three to five letters of recommendations, and teaching evaluations. The job is on a "without salary" basis: in case you didn't catch it the first time, "Applicants must understand there will be no compensation for this position."[10]

Caitlin DeAngelis, an historian on a postdoctoral fellowship at Harvard, taught an undergraduate seminar on—what else—"Harvard and Slavery" for a salary of $0.00. Zero percent adjuncts eat prestige.

5.2.2 Dark Money: Tutoring

Tutoring is the adjunct[11] to adjuncting, the para-academia that lets me believe I can afford its leather briefcases. I spend what I earn, a virtuous circle and vicious cycle.

From one of the companies I work for, I accept a prospective student,

---

10 Anemona Hartocollis, "Help Wanted: Adjunct Professor, Must Have Doctorate. Salary: $0," *The New York Times,* 6 April 2022.

11 See Annie Barnes, "Dark Academia, Dark Money," *Dark Academia* cluster, *Post45,* 15 Mar 2022.

even though I am about to teach my actual class. The father is named "John Sr." and the son is named "John Jr." and they want help on their essay due in seventy-two hours. I get an email from John:

I got Covid recently and have been very sick and sleeping a lot so I haven't done the readings yet and I also missed the lectures relevant to the course. I also am studying for a major midterm in the hardest computer science course so I need your help.

Do you mind if you can help "teach" me the course and create lecture notes and we can together outline the paper? I will send you the materials, readings, prompts etc.

Not to be rude but do you know Hamlet?

Because I am checking my email *while* teaching I don't really look at it, I tell him to call me tonight, which is late, as I commute deep into the witching hour. He rings as though he's tracking me, as soon as I arrive home, *doomed for a certain term to walk the night.*

The father says that he wants someone to synthetize the lectures and also give the son a topic and an outline and really he'll work on this for a solid twenty-four hours, not plagiarism, but like, just up to the edge. When I check the email, it's not the son, the son has been nowhere, it's the father writing as the son.

My pay scale is very high but the tatters of ethics still shroud me. I tell him I will edit the essay if the son comes to me with a topic, also has he asked his professors for an extension if he has Covid?

"He's too proud to ask for an extension, he won't do it," says Old Hamlet. "There are—mental issues. Depression. My psychiatrist is worried about the texts my son is sending to me."

"I can help him brainstorm his topic and edit an essay he's working on," I chirp-croak, it's almost midnight.

"You can't give me what I want," he says, and the phone cuts out of the porches of my ears. *Adieu adieu adieu* and I won't even get paid for this labor that I only do to get paid.

I had a dream that you were letting one of your tutoring clients hypnotize you, writes a friend, who is also a tutor. *You were doing it for a very funny reason but I cannot remember what it was.*

6. CRITICISM

Dark academia is very, very white. White as a gaslit glass of milk.[12] White people love to tell themselves they are doing something about it. *So Eurocentric*,[13] say Martin and Amanda and Helen and Diana and Spencer and Michael and Graham and Brooke. *No representation.* The smugness of whiteness in dark academia. The complacency. If we point something out, then we don't have to do anything about it. If we *name* it and cast our *shame* about it, then we've done what we could do.

Rooted in conservative, elite ideals. Dark academia reifies letter writing and tweedy blazers and glasses and pub names like the Speckled Bantam or Thistle & Jig or Centaur & Pistol, but with the embrace of tartan comes a dark aftertaste of hierarchical gender roles. No fatness. No people of low

---

12 Cf. the films *Notorious* (dir. Alfred Hitchcock) and *Get Out* (dir. Jordan Peele) for the long arc of the whiteness of milk. Cf. also breast milk.

13 For several examples, see "Cultural Dark Academia," sappylittlebitch.tumblr.com

socioeconomic or cultural capital.[14]

Not so.

Moreover, as dark academia scholar Mel Monier argues,[15] to whitewash dark academia is also to ignore the Black artists and writers who are at the vibe's vanguard.

Dark academia thrives on institutions and celebrates the storied moneyed elitism that made it so.

But the institutions are crumbling. Rome is burning. And dark academia is the Emperor Nero,[16] fiddling while he lights the flame.

This article about Dark Academia is a stub. You can help Wikipedia by expanding it.

---

14 Dr. Sarah Burton's lecture at Newcastle University highlights these not-so-latent oversights: see Sarah Burton, "Dark Academia, Gender, Intellectualism," *Newcastle University*, 16 Feb 2021.

15 Mel Monier, "Too Dark for Dark Academia?," *Dark Academia* cluster, *Post45*, 15 Mar 2022.

16 Caffè Nero.

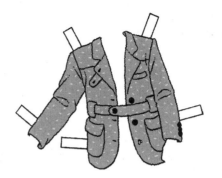

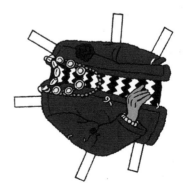

CORONA II

This is the way the world ends
This is the way the world ends
This is the way the world ends
Not with a bang but a post-nasal drip

The things I've bought myself online again:
Drain Weasel, pulse oximeter, so much gum,
I cheat and add a book, so the ones who pack it know
And are impressed at what I chew.
I hate-like everything.
I don't get it, I don't get it, but I've got it.
The sinus infection was negative,
Negative, negative, positive,
On the Day of Daring. Duck, duck, go.
I take the test at midnight, take it twice,
In two different brands. Tell everyone I know
Even though I've seen no one for days,
I tell them in the hopes I'd had a life,

I want someone to panic for: a life.
Everyone's so kind but no one cares.
No close contacts. Been in glasses for two years.
I drink the goo the stars tell me to drink,
Lypospheric Vitamin C, it comes
In thirty little condom packs, you splooge one
Into a shot of water and bolt it down
All in one go. So gross you know it's working.
I wear my duck-bill mask and did I mention I'm alone.
The things I find in the organic bodega:
Elderberry tonic, honey thistle

More honey, fruited bodies, bamboo toilet rolls,
Ginger, lemon, tulsi tea, throat coat,
Turmeric, green minerals, honey rose.

I knew I was seeing it rose-tinted.
I knew it was all going well too fast.
Got invited to a lit-world revel
I'd dreamed about for years, already knew
In the back of my throat. Pretended it could be so.
Can I produce a negative in a day
Can I run Boston in a week
Wake up and feel insultingly fine.
The Face Shield lab technician, weary pink,
Sticks in a wand to snake the Covid out.
I give up on the revel, cling to marathon,
I cannot give all up at once.
Three positives, one day. Not pregnant—I bleed
For the first time in two years.

For the first time in two years, I'd tried to date,
Kissed someone, he was short, it didn't take.
I figured out the outdoor dining early,
Says the silver-haired psychiatrist
I then blind-dated. The first two times, A- / B+.
The third date he invited himself inside.
I knew he was so wrong as soon as he made fun
Of all the friends who lived inside my Peloton.
He told me how good he looked inside his clothes.
What was this person doing in my womb.
I like girls who are too thin to be

Psychologically healthy, he said, three hours
Into his interior monologue.
How do I leave when he's invited himself inside?

Good evening, Adrienne, says the screen inside
The hotel room inside the picture in my phone
On April Fool's, the Day of Dignity.
The hotel, apparently, has accidentally
Inserted another ex into my room,
So he's inside my body before I have arrived,
And texts me a picture of the television screen
Inviting me to already be where I have been before.
Make this journey even more rewarding.
A fire burns in the fireplace on the screen.
He still has a girlfriend, who isn't me.
I swear I didn't plan it, I swear, says he,
But if you want to come? I do. I don't,
But six days later my body is alive.

On the Day of No Nonsense we're back and live. I drive
A block and pop—the tire's out.
A man yells at me, muted through the mask
And through the glass. *Your tire's out.*
But there's a flat fix just around the bend.
I clutch the wheel like I am made of blood,
Judder the thudding car across the road.
One hundred twenty-five to fix. The ATM
Dials the moon to get the cash. He could have said
Your firstborn—I would have had one just to pay.
I would have paid him anything at all.

I drive, I park, I print, I teach, I change
Into my costume for the barre thing that I take
Between the teaching, I don't have a body. I shake

So I don't have to think. Shake, shake.
It's not just me, our phones ding not quite in sync
Tornado Warning, This Is Not A Drill,
We're stronger than we think. When barre is done
Like nothing's happened, we walk into a different sky.
Flat fix to flash flood. Five minutes before class:
Dear Professor Hi! This is your student
I'm excited to meet you! It says
Shelter in place but should we come to class?
I am in the building, so are half,
And so I go to hybrid on the fly
Where I teach at night already in the basement.
In one of the Zoom rooms, the screen goes dark.
Sorry we have a bat in our room, says the cloud.

That next morning's sky is cloudless blue,
Which is even more dangerous of course.
All the roads in Princeton proper have been spared
But every major artery is clogged
With rivers that are rising still.
Allow extra time for your commute.
I run and the tow path is a river
I get a green juice and some nuts,
Wait it out, set to drive at noon,
Everywhere flooded and the one main road
That Google thinks is open is a standstill clog of cars

I fiddle with the car and idle, I give up
Three hours later, try again, three hours later
I am in New York. The sky lingers blue.

The sky today of course is super blue,
Honestly I feel fine, magic, even
My nose is sparkly, very clean
Sparkly is a very Covid feeling. The new
New Coke is Covid. Scrub Daddy. Chlorinated sinuses.
On my third day I didn't know I had it,
That was on the Day of Excess,
I went out running in the sun. Three blocks in,
A freaky hailstorm rent across the sky.
A schlubby guy, Coke-bottle glasses, came out
Of a basement hobbit hole to snap a pic.
The ground was very slick, with sudsy clods
Of hail still glomming up the throat.

I open the Drain Weasel and stick it down my throat,
Swab it in a big circle five times
And then swab again the other way
Sing Happy Birthday to myself, that's how
I know I've done enough, and hock
A Satan-strength dreadlock of viral load.
I stick the snake up my nostril
And peel out my brains like an orange
All in one go. Cara Cara. Sumo.
More Manuka, now in elderberry flavor
I did the elderberry dummies. Didn't help.
I stuck my finger, waited for my breath,

I simply couldn't grade ever again
In this my Covid-addled brain.

In the Great Brain Robbery,
Applicants must understand there will be no compensation.
Both parents got their boomer quad boosters,
Everyone got neonatal immunity,
I'm empty, zero-sum womb
With students in the waiting room
Languishing in their antechambers
If everyone's in breakout is anyone.
This spring's holidays congest together,
Passover, Ramadan, Good Friday, Easter Sunday.
My mom says she caught it over the phone
From me. I'm not even sacrificial.
Little lamb, little lamb, who made thee,
A little more than kinder, less surprise.

When I lived in the toxic house, surprise mold
Seeped from the bathroom stall to wherever else goes mold,
Baseboard, attic, lungs. The other women in that house
Called themselves a coven, fought, laughed, fucked,
Still talk daily, in my head, but not to me.
One time all four separate cartons of eggs
Had progressed somewhere past their best by dates.
Am I not woman if I do not bleed enough?
If Tuesday is Day Zero, it's Day of Consequence.
If you have two legs, run (my Teledoc says, fine!).
If you have one leg, hop. If you have no legs, go.
Day One, the Day of the Experimenter—

Nothing is insignificant. Weakness,
Tempur-Pedic, overwrought.

I went to bed with overwrought muscles
Even for me, my quads ache gently all the time
But woke up in the middle of the night
Spasming in sharp gold blades—
I'd never walk again. That kind of nervous damage
Gone electric, the kind that spreads
Like a toxic dye. Pal, radioactive—
This Covid has harvested my data
And it goes haywire in the body, smashing
Every button on the elevator
So the whole wall lights up buttons
And the door has to judder open
On this and every floor, revealing
People to themselves, and the people to the world.

The body is a body and the body is a world.
I'll never walk again. I wake up, Zocdoc
"Physical therapist," I skip the symptom steps,
What is near me on a Saturday
I call, there's no one in til the third office
We don't sync with Zocdoc, says the sec,
But I can get you an appointment Monday first thing. No.
My pathos is braiding itself down to the floor,
Rapunzel, Rapunzel, what do you dread.
Today's the Day of the Policy Makers.
Because I'm nothing if not a great test-taker
I take myself to test for it again.

Then do a Peloton the same time as my brother
And sweat it steady, damned if I am dead.

The things I've bought myself online again:
I want someone to panic for my life.
I knew I was seeing it in rose.
I knew that I could never really date
From the start, empty girl inside.
On the Day of No Nonsense we're back. I live
So I don't have to think. I'm body. I shake.
That next morning's sky is clueless blue.
The sky today is super glue.
I open the Drain Weasel and stick it down my throat,
Peel the brain to cryptic core.
I judder in the bed, so overbought.
The body keeps the body and this body is a fraud.
I'm home. I'm ready. I'm damned but not yet dead.

ACKNOWLEDGMENTS

Thank you to the following publications, where some of these poems first appeared: *The New Yorker* ("Corona"), *The Paris Review* ("Felix By Proxy"), and *Two Peach* ("Wednesday").

Thank you first and foremost to writing group: Rawaan Alkhatib, Sara Deniz Akant, Ashley Colley, Callie Garnett, Katie Fowley, Dan Poppick, Colby Somerville, and Bridget Talone. Thank you, as well, to Dan Chiasson, Jess Laser, Emily Liebowitz, Jenny Mackenzie, Elizabeth Phillips, Brian Pietras, Mariam Rahmani, Emily Silk, Christopher Spaide, Teresa Trout, Lindsay Turner, and Shannon Winston, among so many others, who provided feedback and support along the way.

Thank you especially to Sara Deniz Akant, for living in the comments.

Thank you to Ilya Milstein for making the dolls come to life.

Infinite gratitude to Caryl Pagel, Alyssa Perry, Daniel Khalastchi, Sevy Perez, and everyone at Rescue Press for your brilliance, wisdom, generosity, adaptability, and magic.

Thank you, always and forever, to my family: Bennett Raphel and Jennifer Finkle; Neil Raphel and Janis Raye. I love you very much.